I SEE STRENGTH IN YOU

by Monica Sheri Scott

"Nevertheless [Lord] I am continually with you; you hold my right hand. You guide me with your counsel, and afterward you will receive me with honor. Whom have I in heaven but you? And there is nothing on earth that I desire other than you. My flesh and my heart may fail, but God is the strength of my heart and my portion forever." Psalm 73:26 NRSV

You are stronger than you think, but unfortunately, sometimes that strength in you will be poured out and spent in great measure. It's in those moments, and the weary moments that follow after, when the Lord is nearest as the strength of your heart. It's there, your devotion as stated in Psalm 73 is deepened. Suffering is temporal, our heart and flesh may fail, but God is eternal, his love is our supply forever.

I hope these notes lift you, shine a light for you, and put some extra confidence and conviction in your next steps. **And when you read these words, I pray you hear them whisper back - I see strength in you.**

Written and published in thanks to every loved one whose encouragement called to me in the storm, "I see you, don't give up!". My debt of gratitude I'm afraid can never be paid in full, but I will pay it forward in your honor for the rest of my life and to the best of my ability. - *Monica*

Dedicated to my children; one day you will understand my loves how in those days you watched me, sat with me, danced with me, prayed with me, and fought with me through devastatingly hard times. I want you to know what got me through. When no one knew but God, like a river in the desert his Word and presence was enough. When the grief was so heavy it felt like the earth was going to swallow me up, the Truth and the Love of God held me. When I felt helpless and hopeless in the darkest night, you two gave me the will to keep walking in the light! And when I had nothing left to give, God sent help to fill my heart and to hold up my arms; so that I could continue to fill your heart and hold you.

Naomi and Boston, no matter how big the mountain - your feet can climb it one step at a time. You've got this, and God's got you. And perhaps the most important truth; just like the people who felt called to our side to help, love, and encourage us - you are called to help, love, and encourage others. This is our purpose; this is your purpose - give it your all! Always and forever believing in you and cheering you on! - *Mommy*

For our struggle is not against enemies of blood and flesh, but against the rulers, against the authorities, against the cosmic powers of this present darkness, against the spiritual forces of evil in the heavenly places. Therefore, take up the whole armor of God, so that you may be able to withstand on that evil day, and having done everything, to stand firm. Ephesians 6:12-13 NRSV

Out of the ashes of our deepest fears and troubles we CAN see our greatest strength building and overcoming. Like anything worth doing, we will not lay hold of it without a healthy dose of struggle and resistance, which require a firm and active approach from us. Out of our hearts grow all the issues of life. Out of our hearts we struggle in the fight for light, heavenly ways, for strength to do and to stand. God is well able to equip and empower you for His work of ministry in the earth, to show his power and glory! Keep building no matter what, you are not in this fight alone.

Then shall the young women rejoice in the dance, and the young men and the old shall be merry. I will turn their mourning into joy, I will comfort them, and give them gladness for sorrow. Jeremiah 31:13 NRSV

As my mom taught me, "Let the joy of the Lord be your strength! Rise up and be strong!" I thank God for people who are able and willing to speak the straight up truth with gracious faith. It's a rare thing, but it's the standard we're all called to, truth and faith. It's not a soul striving work, it's a work of surrender and receiving. It is God who is able to turn our mourning into dancing, who is able to comfort the inconsolable, to give gladness to sorrowful souls. He is able to make all grace abound to you. Yet, it is the will and power of every heart to surrender to Him and his ways, to receive his gifts of righteousness, joy, and peace in the Spirit. Choose him, choose joy.

For it is God who said, "Let light shine out of darkness," who has shone in our hearts to give the light of the knowledge of the glory of God in the face of Jesus Christ. 2 Corinthians 4:6 NRSV

Are you anxious at times? Me too. In the light of the knowledge of the glory of God there is peace. A practice and discipline that helps let the light in and calm MY soul is; first to take deep breathes in a rhythm (exercise forces me to do this as well); then remind myself that the deep negative emotions will pass; next I imagine a place of peace and rest with God; then I acknowledge a blessing of God right in front of me (my children, home, dog, my Bible, something); after that I often call somebody - talk specifically in detail about what is making me anxious and allow them to speak to it; and then finally if need be, I do it all over again! Living in the light doesn't always feel "natural", but it's in you and calling to you in the knowledge of God and in the face Jesus!

True Freedom

IS BEING ABLE TO CHOOSE WHAT

is right

IN SPITE OF _____.

Galatians 5:1

For freedom Christ has set us free. Stand firm, therefore, and do not submit again to a yoke of slavery. Galatians 5:1 NRSV

You are stronger and freer than you feel! Often, it's not BEING trapped that debilitates us, it's the FEELING that we are trapped even when there is way of escape available. The Word of God says, and I believe to be true that when it comes to sin and temptation (i.e. anything not born of faith), God always provides a way of escape from it. So, whatever the next right thing to do is…you can do it! Whether it's to be bold, stay silent, make your bed, call a friend, go for a walk, resist temptation, make a plan, etc... you can do it! This freedom is yours.

It is Christ Jesus, who died, yes, who was raised, who is at the right hand of God, who indeed intercedes for us. Who will separate us from the love of Christ? Will hardship, or distress, or persecution, or famine, or nakedness, or peril, or sword? As it is written, "For your sake we are being killed all day long; we are accounted as sheep to be slaughtered." No, in all these things we are more than conquerors through him who loved us. For I am convinced that neither death, nor life, nor angels, nor rulers, nor things present, nor things to come, nor powers, nor height, nor depth, nor anything else in all creation, will be able to separate us from the love of God in Christ Jesus our Lord. Romans 8:34-39 NRSV

This is a tough one, because no one wants the innocent to suffer. Yet, when life out of our control is painful or hard, our greatest responsibility is to teach those watching to live in it or through it well! In all our suffering, change, and pain; show them we are more than conquerors through Jesus who loves us. Living well, loved and loving IS best for your own good, but it is also the responsibility of Christians for those whose eyes watching in our homes, online, and yes, on our phones. Your actions matter, and perhaps even more your responses to life matter. Stay strong.

See to it that no one fails to obtain the grace of God; that no root of bitterness springs up and causes trouble, and through it many become defiled. Hebrews 12:15 NRSV

Through it all keep your heart and mind grounded in the grace and mercy of God. Release the irrational fears, release the pain, release the blame, release the outcome and simply take responsibility for what's in your hand. It's a problem, but it's also your brave opportunity! You were created with a beautiful mind and heart, don't let it become defiled because of bitterness and fear. The weeds will grow as far you leave them untended. Guard your heart. You've got this!

IF God
is allowing it...
He has a...
PURPOSE
FOR IT

Romans 8:27-28

Likewise, the Spirit helps us in our weakness; for we do not know how to pray as we ought, but that very Spirit intercedes with sighs too deep for words. And God, who searches the heart, knows what the mind of the Spirit is, because the Spirit intercedes for the saints according to the will of God. We know that all things work together for good for those who love God, who are called according to his purpose. Romans 8:26-28 NRSV

God is able to use all the broken pieces of your life for your good and to His glory! He in fact, delights in doing so. His purpose, plans, and promises for life will prevail! In this world we have trouble, because it's a broken and fallen world, but TAKE HEART He has overcome the world. The sovereignty of God in times of trouble is a mystery that we cannot allow to tamper with the clear revealed Truth; He is a good and loving Father, He is near, He will bring us through! He will work things together for your good!

You Have more
- LIFE - to live
- STRENGTH - to spend
- LOVE - to give

Romans 5:5

DO NOT GIVE UP !!

We also boast in our sufferings, knowing that suffering produces endurance, and endurance produces character, and character produces hope, and hope does not disappoint us, because God's love has been poured into our hearts through the Holy Spirit that has been given to us. Romans 5:3-5 NRSV

The lies of fear say, this is the end, it's over, there is no hope, only emptiness. The truth of faith says, suffering produces endurance, character, and hope; because God's love is our source. No matter the need or the problem, I am one hundred percent confident that the source of all answers and provisions are in the Love of God. It is the well of life that never runs dry. Pause, consider your sufferings in light of Love, and then live it out; receive it, hold it, give it!

When the disciples heard this, they were greatly astounded and said, "Then who can be saved?" But Jesus looked at them and said, "For mortals it is impossible, but for God all things are possible." Matthew 19:25-26

We get weary, but we cannot forget that what we see as impassable is possible with God! IT IS (STINKING) POSSIBLE! God can do all things; no purpose of His can be thwarted. I cannot understand His ways, the allowance of certain pains and joys, these are things too mysteriously wonderful for me to know. Builders of this world may reject the ways of God in the wake of their weariness, but Truth still says, the stone the builders rejected will be the cornerstone. His presence will be our strength, salvation, redemption. Hold on to hope!

Shun youthful passions and pursue righteousness, faith, love, and peace, along with those who call on the Lord from a pure heart. Have nothing to do with stupid and senseless controversies; you know that they breed quarrels.
2 Timothy 2:22-23 NRSV

There's no mincing Paul's words here; "Stupid and senseless controversies"! For every conflict or controversy we face internally within ourselves, or externally with others there is a healthy response and a great opportunity for growth. Have you knowingly sinned? There is a healthy response. Have you been sinned against? There is a healthy response. Ignorantly missed a mark? There is a healthy response. Loose your temper? There is a healthy response. Isolated and lonely? There is a healthy response. Worried? There is a healthy response and opportunity to grow through it all. Chin up, you've got this!

For the Lord is good; his steadfast love endures forever, and his faithfulness to all generations. Psalm 100:5 NRSV

When life feels upended it is such a comfort to know our God and king is faithful, enduring and steady. I love those words "his steadfast love endures", "his faithfulness to all generations". In the end love endures and wins. In the end, faithfulness is proven to all generations. God does not change with the shifting of seasons or problems, he remains, he is faithful, he endures! Let his steadiness, steady you. Let his faithfulness strengthen your faithfulness. Let his enduring love give your love endurance. You've come too far to give up now!

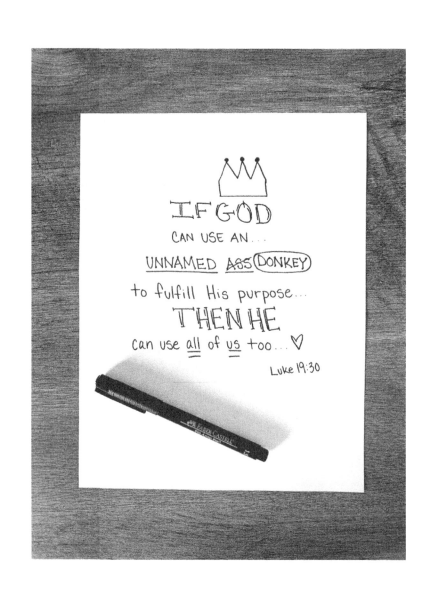

Go into the village ahead of you, and as you enter it you will find tied there a colt that has never been ridden. Untie it and bring it here. If anyone asks you, 'Why are you untying it?' just say this, 'The Lord needs it.' - Jesus Luke 19:30-31 NRSV

It wasn't just that Jesus said to go get the colt, it's that he said he "needed it". It was part of the fulfillment of His Word. How much more is every man and woman today needed for the fulfillment of His Word? It's a great big world out there. It's tempting to see needs as too big to make a difference or to see problems as too big to solve, and yet we were created and given breath to make a difference, to have purpose, to love and be loved! You are more valuable and important than you may think. We can't do everything, but we can do something. What might that be today?

And going a little farther, he threw himself on the ground and prayed, "My Father, if it is possible, let this cup pass from me; yet not what I want but what you want." Matthew 26:39 NRSV

The contrast of the setting here is startling to me. In a beautiful garden, but in the dark. Surrounded by friends, but completely alone. Stress to the point of sweating blood, but in the presence of God. It is possible (and not a sin) to feel at a loss, in the dark, alone, and suffering; AND simultaneously be right smack in the middle of God's love, in the middle of a victory moment, in the middle of God's goodness! Distress comes, but His cup is our victory! You can do this!

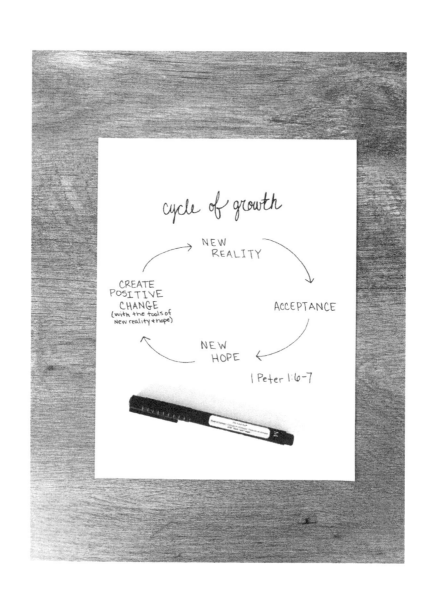

In this you rejoice, even if now for a little while you have had to suffer various trials, so that the genuineness of your faith—being more precious than gold that, though perishable, is tested by fire—may be found to result in praise and glory and honor when Jesus Christ is revealed. 1 Peter 1:6-7 NRSV

From various trials, testing, and refining of our faith – to the praise, glory, and honor of God. It's quit a journey we are on. No matter where, how far, or how long you get knocked down for...keep getting back up, keep pressing forward, keep problem solving, keep the faith, keep growing to the praise, glory, and honor of Jesus name. You are precious to God, the faith in you is precious and worth preserving, protecting, and fighting for!

KEEP TRUSTING   KEEP PRAYING

Maybe God isn't "not" answering your prayers...

→ maybe He is answering them in a way you didn't imagine or prefer.

→ maybe He is waiting on you to do what you know is right + needed of you.

→ maybe He is being patient with another person involved + you need to allow Him to sustain you in the waiting.

Luke 23:47-49 + 2 Peter 3:8-9

When the centurion saw what had taken place, he praised God and said, "Certainly this man was innocent." And when all the crowds who had gathered there for this spectacle saw what had taken place, they returned home, beating their breasts. But all his acquaintances, including the women who had followed him from Galilee, stood at a distance, watching these things.' Luke 23:47-49 NRSV

At the cross where Jesus gave it all; one saw a miracle, some saw defeat, and some watched, wondered, and waited. Their perspectives didn't change the outcome, but it most certainly changed their lives, if nothing else for the days in "the waiting". Let this be a reminder to choose your perspective thoughtfully and to trust the miracle worker, counselor & strengthener, sustainer and provider! Wait in hope, because he's working in you and in others. "The Lord is not slow about his promise, as some think of slowness, but is patient with you, not wanting any to perish, but all to come to repentance." 2 Peter 3:9 NRSV

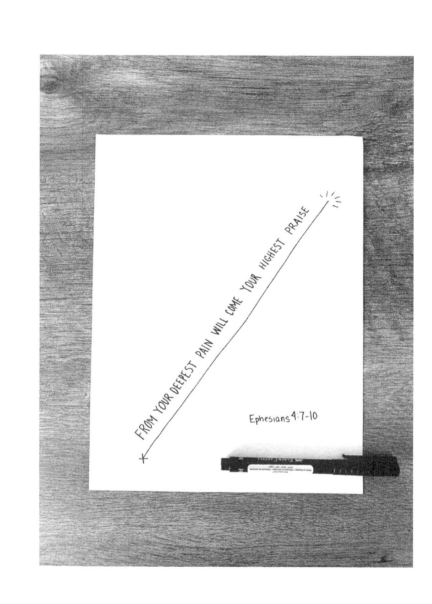

Each of us was given grace according to the measure of Christ's gift. Therefore it is said, "When he ascended on high he made captivity itself a captive; he gave gifts to his people." (When it says, "He ascended," what does it mean but that he had also descended into the lower parts of the earth? He who descended is the same one who ascended far above all the heavens, so that he might fill all things.) Ephesians 4:7-10 NRSV

The Lord descended to the depths to take "captivity" captive, and ascending he gave the gifts of mercy and grace to his people. From the lowest lows, to the highest highs His grace is sufficient. *Thank you, thank you Jesus, from our depths to our heights you are worthy. You overcame in the depths so that we could be over-comers, to the praise and glory of our good God! We trust You from pain to praise!*

Trust in the Lord with all your heart, and do not rely on your own insight. In all your ways acknowledge him, and he will make straight your paths. Proverbs 3:5-6 NRSV

Trust gives God the ability to make what looks like crooked trails into straight paths if and when we trust, rely, and acknowledge him in our ways and actions. Get His wisdom from the Word, trust his ways, acknowledge him in the choices and turns, and keep moving forward. Little by little, step by step you are making progress, you are making a difference in the world around you. Rest your soul regularly, rest physically regularly, but don't you dare get stagnant – we need you! Keep plodding on!

He said to me, "Do not fear, Daniel, for from the first day that you set your mind to gain understanding and to humble yourself before your God, your words have been heard, and I have come because of your words. Daniel 10:12 NRSV

I love the image of God inclining his ear and presence toward humility and understanding. Humility and meekness are not the absence of power, they are power under control or better yet power in submission; to God, His wisdom, timing, Word, & direction. I've seen bad things happen to good people A LOT and I cannot understand why, but no matter how many bad things happen to truly humble hearts I see them rise with peace and joy! The Lord has and will have the final word on everything! Blessed are the meek, they will inherit the earth, Jesus said. I don't know who needs to hear this, but stay humble in the presence of God and man, remember the promise.

The fear [awe] of the Lord is the beginning of wisdom, and the knowledge of the Holy One is insight. Proverbs 9:10 NRSV

This one's really just for those of us that feel the tension between unhealthy fear and godly wisdom - I'm sure it's just a few! (Ha) No, this is a soul check for us all. What thoughts or feelings of fear are you wrestling with? They are worth inspecting and interviewing. We are not battling against flesh and blood. No, this is a spiritual battle we fight, and we are transformed by the renewing of our minds. What are you afraid of? Where is God calling you to be brave, to surrender to him, to fight, to rest? Only you and God can have this conversation. Go for it!

Jesus said, 'How can you believe (in me) when you accept glory from one another and do not seek the glory that comes from the one who alone is God?' John 5:44 NRSV

The glory of love is altogether intoxicating, but only the real thing is fulfilling. The counterfeit of giving or taking from others the glory and faith that belongs to God alone will always lead to emotional injury on all parties involved. But glory given to God, AND equality-based love-connections shared with others will result in peace. You exist to be interconnected not objectified for admiration, glory, or power. Guard your heart fam, you are truly, REAL-ly and deeply loved!

Faithful	Faithful
Faithful	Fruitful ☼
Faithful	Faithful
Faithful	Faithful
Faithful	Faithful
Fruitful ✿	Faithful
Faithful	Fruitful
Faithful	...Don't give up now!
Faithful	
Fruitful ♡	John 15:4-5
Faithful	James 3:17

Jesus said, "Abide in me as I abide in you. Just as the branch cannot bear fruit by itself unless it abides in the vine, neither can you unless you abide in me. I am the vine, you are the branches. Those who abide in me and I in them bear much fruit, because apart from me you can do nothing." John 15:4-5 NRSV

Picture it, imagine yourself as that branch grafted into the vine, choosing to remain. Imagine the day that the fruit reveals itself, it'll be worth the wait. Faithfully, patiently and intentionally stay connected to him; enduring the seasons, receiving, remaining, waiting for the fruit. FRUIT IS COMING! FRUIT. IS. COMING! You can do this!

We are called to be
PEACE 'MAKERS'
not
PEACE 'KEEPERS'!

James 3:17-18

But the wisdom from above is first pure, then peaceable, gentle, willing to yield, full of mercy and good fruits, without a trace of partiality or hypocrisy. And a harvest of righteousness is sown in peace for those who make peace. James 3:17-18 NRSV

Jesus also said, blessed are the peace makers, for they will be called sons or daughters of God. Peace 'keepers' passively or passive aggressively try to keep the peace at the expense of what is right. On the other hand, peace 'makers' pursue peace without sacrificing truth or grace. Sadly, this 'God idea' of peace-making can often run counter to what many are taught concerning Christian character, femininity, and honor. Peace-making is not passive, dismissive, fearful, ignorant, or weak. Peace-making is rarely comfortable and rarely without conflict, but it is good, beautiful, and right! Pursue peace, don't settle for "keeping the peace" or "faking the peace". You can do it!

Happy are those who do not follow the advice of the wicked, or take the path that sinners tread, or sit in the seat of scoffers; but their delight is in the law of the Lord, and on his law they meditate day and night. They are like trees planted by streams of water, which yield their fruit in its season, and their leaves do not wither. In all that they do, they prosper. Psalm 1:1-3 NRSV

In my home, often with kid messes of all kinds, I have been known to ask visiting guests to please not mind my mess. I ask for approval of my mess and everyone is usually obliged to give it! That is very gracious of guests in my home, but that is not a healthy way to live our whole lives. We should mind some messes in our heart and in our lives. The "awareness of messes" should affect where and who we follow, where and when we sit and let our guard down. I actually think this is what Paul talked about when he said don't be unequally yoked, being careful of whose steps, path, and model we follow. So yes, in your heart and life mind the mess. Also, there is a pretty amazing promise tied to those who delight in the Lord and "his way". May it be yours!

The thief comes only to steal and kill and destroy. I came that they may have life, and have it abundantly. "I am the good shepherd. The good shepherd lays down his life for the sheep. The hired hand, who is not the shepherd and does not own the sheep, sees the wolf coming and leaves the sheep and runs away—and the wolf snatches them and scatters them. The hired hand runs away because a hired hand does not care for the sheep. I am the good shepherd. I know my own and my own know me, just as the Father knows me and I know the Father. And I lay down my life for the sheep. John 10:10-15 NRSV

The evil one comes to steal, kill, and destroy. The good Shepard comes that we might have life abundantly. The evil one takes, isolates, and corrupts. The good Shepard protects, leads, and corrects. Shame is self-focused and self-consuming; all be it self-destructive. Discipleship is self-denying and self-sacrificing; all be it self-building. Lord, I pray we know your voice, know the difference between conviction and shame, open the eyes of our hearts.

EQUALITY is KEY TO EMPATHY.

For those who think too highly or too little of self.

Galatians 3:26-29

For in Christ Jesus you are all children of God through faith. As many of you as were baptized into Christ have clothed yourselves with Christ. There is no longer Jew or Greek, there is no longer slave or free, there is no longer male and female; for all of you are one in Christ Jesus. Galatians 3:26-28 NRSV

Jesus came and leveled the field of equality in Him; it says he leveled it for race, power and status, and for gender. In Him we are all children of God, we are one. As long as we see each other as "better than, less than", "victim and oppressor", "power over, ignorant lower" we will miss the blessings of empathy, compassion, and love; peace. Sometimes these false perceptions of ourselves and others are easy to glaze over; I believe that's why David prayed prayers like, "Search me, O God, and know my heart; test me and know my thoughts. See if there is any wicked way in me, and lead me in the way everlasting (Psalm 139:23-24) Let this be our prayer as well!

For I am convinced that neither death, nor life, nor angels, nor rulers, nor things present, nor things to come, nor powers, nor height, nor depth, nor anything else in all creation, will be able to separate us from the love of God in Christ Jesus our Lord. Romans 8:38-39 NRSV

This fact cannot be changed.
Life, circumstances, negative words and actions cannot change it.
Rejection from heights of leadership, peers, or self cannot change it.
Nothing can separate you from God's love in Jesus. You are wanted and precious to Him. Know the truth, let it set you free to be and to be loved. You are his beloved.
Beloved, BE LOVED!

O God, you are my God, I seek you, my soul thirsts for you; my flesh faints for you, as in a dry and weary land where there is no water. So I have looked upon you in your sanctuary, beholding your power and glory. Because your steadfast love is better than life, my lips will praise you.
Psalm 63:1-3 NRSV

Your feelings are not there to create reality or truth, they are not thoughts or ideas. Feelings, specifically negative feelings are signals, bright flashing arrows pointing to your brain, to your mind, "Look here, something is wrong here, a belief or thought is off and needs attention." It's not the sign itself that needs help, no, it's what's lying beneath it! God's love is life - abundant life water, it's the answer to the thirst of your soul, the answer to the problem that lies beneath. Seek Him, and you will find him today!

The integrity of the upright guides them, but the crookedness of the treacherous destroys them. Proverbs 11:3 NRSV
We intend to do what is right not only in the Lord's sight but also in the sight of others. 2 Corinthians 8:21 NRSV

People say integrity is what you do when no one is watching, but the truth is someone is always watching. God is patient, merciful, and gracious. God is justice, righteous, and holy. God is love, and love is ALL those things; not a portion, not a part, not a piece - ALL.
How important is integrity? How important is standing for what is right? How important is it to be a voice for the voiceless? How important is it to ask integrity of those put in places of authority by God and man to administer justice and truth? How important is it that in histories of organized oppression, lies, or abuse, tables of authority are made diverse with sexes, races, and economic status? How important is it that leaders OVER people, not think themselves ABOVE the law or unaccountable for actions or inaction? How important is it for leaders to exert efforts to make right what has been wronged? How important is it that one not bury one's head in order to remain comfortably naive of injustice? How important is authenticity and honesty? How important is your integrity? Everyone sins and falls short, everyone needs the mercy of God, everyone needs accountability, and everyone can be a minister of reconciliation where sin has brought brokenness. You can do this! You can make a difference!

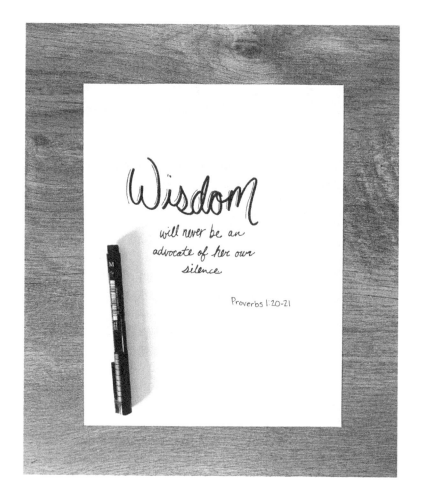

Wisdom cries out in the street; in the squares she raises her voice. At the busiest corner she cries out; at the entrance of the city gates she speaks'. Proverbs 1:20-21 NRSV

Will wisdom advocate for our silence at times, for patience, for appropriate time and place? Absolutely! Wisdom will call for the silence of sin, distractions, misleading words and confusion. Wisdom longs to be heard and is always speaking. It is our job to develop open ears to hear her by having a humbly postured heart, by being courageous to seek the truth, by being open to correction and insight, and by taking responsibility for ourselves. Christ is the wisdom of God manifest, keep Him at the center of your vision of what wisdom and strength looks like. You've got this!

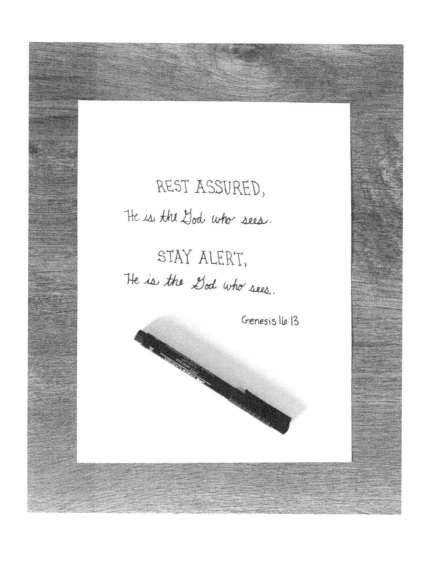

Then she called the name of the Lord who spoke to her, "You are God Who Sees"; for she said, "Have I not even here [in the wilderness] remained alive after seeing Him [who sees me with understanding and compassion]?"'
Genesis 16:13 AMP

Man looks at the most outer appearances; power, status, beauty, money, but God looks at the heart. God can see past our armor, dirt, and anger, and see a son or a daughter. He sees past the masks, facades, and deceptions to the heart of our matters, and He is there - our Hope. So, let the words of your mouth and meditations of your heart be acceptable to the Lord. (Psalm 49:3) Stay aware of the condition of your heart, and rest assured he sees you. You are never alone!

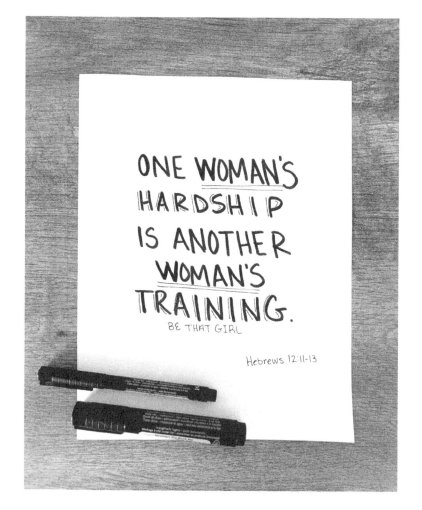

Now, discipline always seems painful rather than pleasant at the time, but later it yields the peaceful fruit of righteousness to those who have been trained by it. Therefore lift your drooping hands and strengthen your weak knees, and make straight paths for your feet, so that what is lame may not be put out of joint, but rather be healed. Hebrews 12:11-13 NRSV

If life was as easy as you wanted, you wouldn't be as strong as you are. So, lift your drooping hands, wield the Spirit of Truth and Love. Strengthen up your weak knees with a holy confidence and conviction. Make straight paths for your feet with wisdom and clarity that come from the Prince of Peace. God is not a God of confusion, but clarity through truth and grace! When we are weak and weary it can feel like the only option is to break; but this (God's way) is the way to not just survive the hardship but even heal through it! There is strength in you yet!

Create your own.

Create your own.

Create your own.

Create your own.

Create your own.

Create your own.

Create your own.

Create your own.

Create your own.

Create your own.

Create your own.

Create your own.

Create your own.

Create your own.

Create your own.

Create your own.

Create your own.

Create your own.

Create your own.

Create your own.

Create your own.

Create your own.

Create your own.

Create your own.

Create your own.

Create your own.

Create your own.

Create your own.

Create your own.

Create your own.

Create your own.

Create your own.

Made in the USA
Monee, IL
15 November 2022

17855794R00056